To

From

Date

Standard
BIBLE STORYBOOK SERIES

JOSEPH AND MOSES

Retold by Carolyn Larsen

PUBLISHING

Cincinnati, Ohio

Published by Standard Publishing, Cincinnati, Ohio
www.standardpub.com
Copyright © 2012 by Standard Publishing

Printed in: China

Project editors: Elaina Meyers, Dawn A. Medill, and Marcy Levering
Cover design: Dale Meyers

Illustrations from Standard Publishing's Classic Bible Art Collection

ISBN 978-0-7847-3524-4

Library of Congress Cataloging-in-Publication Data

Larsen, Carolyn, 1950-
 Joseph and Moses / retold by Carolyn Larsen.
    p. cm.
 ISBN 978-0-7847-3524-4
1. Joseph (Son of Jacob)--Juvenile literature. 2. Moses (Biblical leader)-
-Juvenile literature. 3. Bible stories, English--O.T. Genesis. 4. Bible
stories, English--O.T. Exodus. I. Title.
 BS580.J6L265 2012
 222'.109505--dc23
                              2011051576

17 16 15 14 13 12   1 2 3 4 5 6 7 8 9

THE LIFE OF JOSEPH

Jacob had 12 sons. Of course, he loved all his boys but his favorite son was Joseph, the next to the youngest son. The 10 older boys knew that Joseph was their father's favorite and it made them very jealous. Jacob's favoritism caused Joseph a lot of problems with his brothers. Jacob didn't intend for that to happen, but it did. These problems were a part of God's plan for His people.

A Coat of Many Colors *Genesis 37:1-5*

Jacob and his wives and children returned to the land of Canaan where Jacob's father, Isaac, had lived. Jacob was glad to be home and glad to be away from Laban, the father of his two wives. Laban had cheated him and threatened his life.

Jacob had 12 sons who were very important in God's story. Each of those sons grew up to lead one of the 12 tribes of Israel. Jacob loved all of his sons, but his favorite was Joseph, the next to the youngest son. Part of the reason that Jacob loved Joseph so much was that Joseph was born when Jacob was an old man and he loved Joseph's mother, Rachel, best.

As in any Hebrew family, each of Jacob's sons had jobs to do. Joseph's job, along with some of his brothers, was to watch his father's sheep. But Joseph knew that he was his father's favorite son so he added one little chore to watching the sheep. He also watched his brothers! If his brothers did bad things or misbehaved, Joseph reported it to his father. That made him very unpopular with his brothers. They didn't trust Joseph and they didn't like him at all.

Jacob either didn't notice how his other sons felt or he just didn't care. It seemed like whatever Joseph did just made Jacob love him more. He gave Joseph many gifts that he didn't give his other sons. One day he gave Joseph a very special, beautiful gift. It was a new coat, but not just any coat. This one had many bright and beautiful colors on it. When Joseph wore it, people could see him coming from far away. Each time Joseph's brothers

saw him wearing that coat they were reminded once again of how their father loved him more than any of them. They hated Joseph more and more, especially the oldest brothers who should have been the honored sons in the family. None of them could find a single good thing to say about Joseph. When they were together they talked about how much they hated him.

Joseph's Unusual Dreams *Genesis 37:6-17*

J oseph often got his brothers into trouble because he reported to their dad when they were misbehaving or goofing off. But he wasn't really trying to get them into trouble. He did not seem to know how much they hated him. If he *did* know then he probably would not have done this next thing.

One night Joseph had a dream that was really amazing. Perhaps he should have kept the dream to himself,

but he didn't. He ran and told his brothers the whole thing. "Brothers! Listen to this dream I had. We were all out in a field tying bundles of grain together. All of a sudden, my bundle stood up tall and all of your bundles circled around it and bowed down to it! It was amazing!"

Joseph's brothers were not very happy to hear about this dream. "So, what are you saying? Do you think you're going to be our king?" They made fun of him and laughed at his ridiculous dream. But his dream made them hate him more.

The next night Joseph had another dream which he also reported to his brothers. "This time the sun, moon, and stars bowed down to me!" He told his father about this dream. As much as his father loved Joseph, he didn't appreciate the dream either.

"Are you saying that your mother and I are going to bow down to you?" Jacob asked. Joseph's brothers hated him even more because of this second dream, but Jacob didn't hate him.

Instead, he wondered if the dream had real meaning and what it might be.

Not long after Joseph's two dreams, Jacob sent his other sons to take his flocks to a field near the town of Shechem. They were gone for quite a while and Jacob had heard no reports from them. So he sent Joseph to check on them and report back to him. When Joseph got to Shechem he wasn't exactly sure where to find his brothers and he wandered around from field to field looking for them. A man noticed Joseph and thought that he might be lost so he asked Joseph what he was looking for.

"I'm trying to find my brothers and their flocks," Joseph answered. "Have you seen them anywhere?"

"Yes," the man answered. "I saw them, but they are no longer here. I heard them say they were going to take the flocks to Dothan." So Joseph headed for Dothan to find his brothers. Joseph's life took an unusual turn when he got there.

Joseph Becomes a Slave *Genesis 37:18-36*

Joseph traveled to Dothan to find his brothers so that he could report back to his father how they were doing. Jacob asked him to do that, but Joseph's brothers were not happy to see him. When he was still a long way off, his brothers saw Joseph walking toward them. It was hard to miss his brightly colored coat—a special gift to him from their father. Just seeing that coat again made them angry. So the brothers huddled together and came up with an evil plan. They decided to kill their

brother, Joseph, because their father loved him best and because of his dreams about them bowing down to him. "We can kill him and throw his body into a deep pit, then tell Father that a wild animal ate him." That was their plan. But one brother, Reuben, came to Joseph's rescue. He didn't want his younger brother to be killed.

"Wait, brothers. I don't like this

plan. Why should we have his blood on our souls? Let's just throw him into the pit and let him die on his own. The pit is deep enough that he can't climb out, so eventually he will die without us touching him." Reuben's secret plan was to go back after the brothers had left, rescue Joseph from the pit, and return him to their father. The brothers agreed to Reuben's plan.

When Joseph finally reached them, the brothers grabbed him, pulled off his coat of many colors, and threw him into the deep pit. Joseph cried out for them to help him but they ignored him and sat down to eat. Then one of the brothers noticed a long line of camels off in the distance. It was a group of traders heading to Egypt to sell their spices and perfumes. "Hmmm," Judah said, "listen, we don't really have anything to gain from Joseph dying. We just want him out of our lives, right? What if we sell him to those traders and they take him to Egypt and sell him into slavery? We can still tell Father that a wild animal got him. What do you think?" All the brothers talked about this idea and decided it was a good one because they would be rid of Joseph but they wouldn't have his death on their conscience.

When the traders were nearby the brothers called them over. They sold their brother for 20 pieces of silver and the traders tied him up and took him to Egypt. Reuben, the brother who wanted to free Joseph, was gone when all of this happened. So when he came back to rescue Joseph, he was surprised to find the pit empty. Reuben was very upset and went to find his brothers. With tears rolling down his cheeks he said, "Joseph is gone! What do I do now?"

The brothers already had a plan though. They killed a goat and dipped Joseph's brightly colored coat in the blood. Then they went home and showed the bloody coat to their father. "We found this coat in a field," they lied. "Can you identify it as Joseph's?"

Jacob recognized the coat at once and he was heartbroken. "Yes, it is my son's coat. A wild animal must have eaten him. Joseph must be dead." Jacob was heartbroken and mourned for his favorite son for a long time. The whole family tried to comfort him but he would not listen to any of them. "I will die grieving for my son," he said.

Meanwhile, the group of traders arrived in Egypt and sold Joseph as a slave.

Joseph in Potiphar's House *Genesis 39:1-6*

Joseph must have been very confused as the traders took him from his brothers and began the long trip to Egypt. Why had this happened to him? Why did his brothers do this to him? Did he have any idea how jealous his brothers were of him?

When the traders arrived in Egypt they immediately put Joseph up for sale as a slave. He went from being the favorite son of Jacob to being

a lowly slave. Joseph was a strong, good-looking young boy so he probably brought a good price. A man named Potiphar bought Joseph to be one of his many slaves. Potiphar was the captain of the guard in the king's palace so he was an important, powerful, and rich man.

Joseph was put to work in Potiphar's house doing jobs that he may never have done before. But Joseph didn't complain. He didn't fight what had happened to him, though he must have wondered why his own brothers would do something as terrible as selling him into slavery. Joseph worked hard! He did every job assigned to him as well as he could do it. He was honest and respectful. He did this because God was with him. Joseph gained strength and confidence from knowing that he wasn't alone—God knew what was happening. God blessed Joseph in all he did and Potiphar noticed how hard his new slave worked.

He noticed that Joseph didn't steal things from his house. He saw that Joseph was truthful and showed respect. Joseph quickly became a favorite of Potiphar and was rewarded with a promotion. Potiphar put Joseph in charge of all the slaves who worked in Potiphar's house. Joseph was in charge of the household and all of Potiphar's business deals. He managed everything that happened in the house. He managed the field workers and the workers who took care of the animals. He had a lot of responsibility. This high position showed that Potiphar trusted Joseph with his home, his possessions, and his family. With Joseph in charge, everything in Potiphar's house ran smoothly. His crops and animals did well. Potiphar didn't have to worry about anything. Joseph took care of it all. Things were turning out pretty well for Joseph, but his situation was about to take a turn for the worse.

Joseph Goes to Prison *Genesis 39:19–40:23*

J oseph worked hard as the head slave in Potiphar's house. His master was very pleased with everything Joseph did.

But a problem developed for the young slave. Potiphar's wife began flirting with Joseph. She thought he was very handsome and she wanted

Joseph to do things that he knew were wrong. When Joseph refused to do what she wanted, Potiphar's wife told horrible lies about Joseph to her husband. She accused him of doing the very things he had refused to do! Potiphar was very angry with Joseph so he had him thrown in prison. One minute Joseph was running Potiphar's whole household and the next minute he was in jail. But God was still with Joseph and He helped Joseph be a model prisoner. Joseph worked hard and was always respectful. The jailers noticed Joseph. Before very long, the chief jailer put Joseph in charge of all the other prisoners. The chief jailer's job was much easier because Joseph took care of everything.

A little while later the Egyptian Pharaoh got very upset with his chief cupbearer and his chief baker. He had them thrown in prison and they ended up in the same prison as Joseph. One night the cupbearer and baker both had very disturbing

dreams that they didn't understand. The next day Joseph saw that each of these men seemed to be upset by something. He asked them what was wrong and they each told him they had bad dreams. Joseph asked to hear their dreams and when they told him, God helped him explain the meaning of the dreams. He told the cupbearer that he would be freed from jail and would return to his job as cupbearer to the Pharaoh. Joseph told the baker that he also would be freed from jail but Pharaoh would have him killed. The cupbearer and baker were thankful to know what their dreams meant, but the baker certainly hoped that Joseph was wrong. A short time later both of those men were released from jail, just as Joseph had said they would be. When they were released, the cupbearer was restored to his job for the Pharaoh. But the Pharaoh ordered that the baker be killed, just as Joseph had said. Joseph asked the cupbearer to please remember how he had helped him by interpreting the dream and to help him get released from jail too. But once he was free, the cupbearer forgot all about Joseph.

Joseph Is in Charge! *Genesis 41*

Two years after the cupbearer was released from prison, the Pharaoh of Egypt had a dream that he couldn't understand. It woke him up and he was upset about what it might mean. The Pharaoh fell back asleep and had a second dream that upset him even more. The two dreams bothered him so much that he called in all his wise men, advisers, and magicians and commanded them to interpret the dreams for him. None of them could tell him what the dreams meant.

Just then the cupbearer remembered Joseph. "Pharaoh, when I was in your jail I had a dream that I couldn't understand. There was another prisoner there who told me the exact meaning of my dream. Everything he said came true; for me and also for your chief baker."

Pharaoh sent for Joseph at once. After cleaning up and changing clothes, Joseph came to see the Pharaoh. "I have been told that you can explain dreams," the Pharaoh said to Joseph.

"No," Joseph answered, "that is not completely true. I can't explain your dream, but God can."

That was good enough for Pharaoh, so he told Joseph all about his two dreams. "Both dreams mean the same thing," Joseph said. "They mean that Egypt will have seven good years of many crops and immediately seven years of famine will follow. I think you should choose the wisest man in Egypt and put him in charge of saving and planning for the seven bad years. That way you will have enough food to get your nation through the seven bad years."

Pharaoh thought Joseph's idea was a good one. He met with his advisers to choose a wise man to lead the plan. As they talked, Pharaoh had an idea, "Who would be better than the very man who came up with this plan?" he asked. Pharaoh wanted Joseph in the position! "Joseph, you will manage my palace and organize the people of my land. Only I myself will have more authority than you in all of Egypt." He gave Joseph new clothes and put his own ring on Joseph's finger. Joseph went from being a prisoner to being the second in command in all of Egypt.

So God's plan for Joseph was put into action. For the seven good years Joseph saved and stored food and grain. After seven years the storehouses were filled to overflowing. So when the seven bad years of famine came and people in neighboring nations were starving, Egypt had plenty of food. People from other countries came to Egypt to try to buy food. Every person who came had to speak to Joseph.

Joseph's Family Reunion *Genesis 42; 45:1-15*

Famine struck Egypt and all the lands around it. For seven years no crops would grow and people could not find food anywhere. The news that Egypt had food in its storehouses spread quickly. People came from many nations to ask Joseph if they could buy food. One group of people who came was Joseph's ten older brothers. His

younger brother, Benjamin, stayed home with their father. When the brothers came before Joseph, he recognized them immediately. But they didn't know who Joseph was. They thought their brother was a slave, not a ruler. Joseph pretended not to know who they were. He asked, "Who are you and where have you come from?"

"We are the sons of Jacob and we have come from the land of Canaan to buy grain," the brothers answered.

"No, I know better. I know you are here to spy on my land," Joseph said. Joseph insisted that they were lying. He said he would only believe their story if they went back and got their youngest brother. So he put all the brothers in jail for three days. Then Joseph allowed all of the brothers but one to return to Canaan and get Benjamin. The brothers agreed to do so. As they talked with each other, they thought that this was all happening to them because of what they had done to their brother, Joseph. The brothers didn't know that Joseph, who was listening to them talk, could understand everything they said. He learned that his brothers felt bad about what they did to him. Simeon was the brother chosen to stay behind while the others hurried back to get Benjamin.

Joseph gave them grain to take back to their families. They paid him for the grain, but Joseph had the money put into their bags of grain. They didn't find the money until they stopped for the night on their journey home. They were very frightened that Joseph would think they had stolen the grain so they waited until the grain was gone to return to Egypt.

When the brothers returned with Benjamin, Joseph had another plan. He invited all the brothers to eat with him. The brothers were afraid to go into Joseph's house. As soon as they got inside they confessed to Joseph's servant about the money. "Don't worry," he told them, "your God must have taken care of you. We got our money. That's all that matters." When Joseph came in, he asked the brothers about their father. They assured him that their father was in good health. Then he asked to meet their youngest brother. Joseph was overcome with emotion when he saw Benjamin. He had to leave the room. When he returned, Joseph told the brothers where to sit at the table. They were very surprised when he sat them in the right order—oldest to youngest!

Eventually, Joseph could not keep his secret any longer. "Brothers, I am Joseph. I am the one you sold into slavery!" The brothers were terrified.

They thought Joseph would throw them all into an Egyptian prison. But he promised them that he would not. "You meant evil for me but God turned it into good. He put me into this position so that I could be here to save your lives. Go back to Canaan and get our father. Bring your families here to Egypt so that I can take care of all of you." Joseph kissed each of his brothers, including young Benjamin whom he was thrilled to see.

THE STORY OF MOSES

Joseph's success in Egypt made him very popular with the Pharaoh. Because of him the Hebrew people were protected from problems. But sometime after Joseph died a new Pharaoh came into power. This Pharaoh didn't know anything about Joseph. He didn't know what Joseph had done for Egypt. He was very nervous about all the Hebrews living in his country. He was worried that they might work together and try to take over Egypt. So the Egyptians made the Hebrews their slaves. They were mean slave masters and forced the Hebrew people to make bricks to build their cities. They made them work long hours in the fields. But God hadn't forgotten His people. He had an amazing plan to rescue them.

Moses Is Born and Rescued! *Exodus 2:1-10*

K ill every Hebrew baby boy that is born," the Egyptian Pharaoh ordered. The midwives could let the girl babies live. The Pharaoh didn't want any more Hebrew men in Egypt, so he solved the problem by not allowing more boys to live. But the midwives feared God so they didn't obey the Pharaoh. That made him angry so he ordered his people to grab all the Hebrew boy babies and throw them into the Nile River.

One Hebrew couple from the tribe of Levi had a baby boy during this time. He was a beautiful baby and his mother could not stand the idea of him being killed. She believed God

had great work for him to do. The couple hid the baby in their home for three months and managed to keep him quiet enough that no one knew about him. By then his cries were loud enough that his mother knew he would be discovered. But the brave mother had an idea. She wove a little basket from the tall grasses that grew along the edge of the Nile River. Then she covered the basket with tar so it would be waterproof. She put her precious baby boy in the basket and placed it in the river.

"Stay here and watch what happens to your baby brother," the mother told her daughter, Miriam. The young girl hid nearby and watched the little basket floating in the water.

A little while later the Egyptian princess came down to bathe in the river. She had many servants with her. The princess saw the little basket bobbing in the water and sent one of her servant girls to get it. When she opened the basket the small baby was crying and that touched her heart. "This is a Hebrew baby," she said. The princess decided right then to keep the baby as her own.

Miriam watched this all happening. Then she had an idea. She ran up to the princess and asked, "Would you like me to find a Hebrew woman to care for this baby for you?" The princess thought that was a great idea so Miriam raced back to her own home!

"Mother, come quickly!" Miriam shouted. "The princess has found our baby. She is going to keep him but she wants a Hebrew woman to care for him while he is so young. Come, Mother! You can take care of our baby and he will be safe!"

So the baby's own mother cared for him and the princess never knew that the baby belonged to the nurse-maid. She even paid the mother for her work. When the child was old enough, he went to live in the palace with the princess. She named him *Moses* because that means "drawn out of the water."

God Speaks from a Burning Bush

Exodus 3:1–4:17

Moses' mother was right when she thought God had a special job for her little boy. God saved Moses from Pharaoh for a reason. Moses grew up to become a shepherd. One day he was taking care of his father-in-law's flock of sheep and he took the flock into the wilderness near Mt. Sinai. Moses was watching the sheep eat the grass when suddenly the angel of the Lord called to him. Moses looked around and saw a bush that seemed to be on fire. He was amazed because the bush was burning and burning, but it did not burn up! He walked toward the bush to see if he could figure out what was going on.

"Moses! Moses!" the Lord called to him.

"Here I am," Moses answered.

"Don't come any closer," the Lord said. "Take your sandals off because this is holy ground." Then He said, "I

am the God of your ancestors Abraham, Isaac, and Jacob."

When Moses heard this, he was terrified. He hid his face in his hands because he was afraid to look at God.

"Moses," God said, "I have seen the misery of my people in Egypt. I've heard their cries to be free from the slavery of the Egyptians. I know they have been suffering and I am going to rescue them. I am going to lead them out of Egypt and to their own land. It is the land of Canaan—a wonderful land flowing with milk and honey. Yes, the cries of the people have been heard. I am sending you to talk to Pharaoh. You will lead my people out of Egypt."

"Wait," Moses said, "Who am I to talk to Pharaoh? How can you expect me to lead the Israelites out of Egypt?"

"Don't worry," God said, "I will be with you. Bring the people out of Egypt, then return right to this mountain and worship me."

"But if I go to the people and tell them that God instructed me to lead them out of Egypt, they won't believe me. They will ask what Your name is. What should I tell them?"

"Tell them that I AM has sent you to them. Now go call the leaders of the Israelites together. Tell them that God appeared to you in a burning bush. Tell them that I promise to rescue them from Egypt and lead them to their own land."

Moses wasn't sure that the Israelites would listen to him. So God told him to throw his shepherd's staff down on the ground. When Moses did, God turned it into a snake. Then God told Moses to pick up the snake. When he did, God turned it back into a staff. That showed Moses God's power! "Do this for the people and they will listen to you," God said. Moses still thought the people wouldn't listen to him, so God gave him a few other ways Moses could help them believe. But then Moses said he wasn't sure that he could do what God was asking him to do because he wasn't good at speaking in public. God got a little angry with Moses but He agreed to let Moses' brother, Aaron, go with him. God would speak to Moses. Moses would tell Aaron what God said, then Aaron would speak to Pharaoh and the people.

The Plagues on Egypt *Exodus 7:14–10:29*

Moses and Aaron went to the Egyptian Pharaoh and told him, "The Lord God says, 'Let my people go so they can worship me in the wilderness.'" Pharaoh refused to listen to them. He didn't care at all what God said. It was time for a more direct approach. God told Moses and Aaron to go back to Pharaoh. "Meet him on the banks of the river. Take along your shepherd's staff. Tell Pharaoh that I say he should let my people go! If he refuses again, hit the waters of the river with

your staff. I will turn the water to blood. All the water in Egypt will be blood but the water where you Israelites live will be just fine." God was right; the water turned to blood. But that didn't convince Pharaoh to let the Israelites go.

God sent a second plague on the Egyptian people. He made thousands and thousands of frogs fill the land of Egypt. There were frogs everywhere. The Egyptians couldn't take a step without squishing a frog. But there were no frogs where the Israelites lived. Still Pharaoh would not let the people go.

God wasn't finished with Pharaoh. The third plague happened when Aaron hit the dusty earth with his staff and all the dust turned into gnats. The little bugs flew into mouths, ears, eyes—they were everywhere—except where the Israelites lived. Pharaoh still would not let the people go.

The next plague sent on the Egyptians was flies. Flies were all around. The Egyptian people couldn't take a bite of food without getting flies in their mouths. Still Pharaoh said that the Israelites could not leave.

The fifth plague was against all the livestock the Egyptians owned. Their horses, cows, donkeys, camels, and sheep died. The Israelites' animals were fine. Still Pharaoh would not let God's people leave Egypt.

During the sixth plague, the Egyptians' bodies were covered with painful boils. The people were miserable but Pharaoh would not release the Israelites.

Crops were destroyed with the seventh plague. Hail crashed down on the Egyptians' fields. The eighth plague was on the crops too. Locusts came and ate everything that the hail hadn't destroyed in the fields. Pharaoh still refused to let the Israelites leave.

The ninth plague was darkness. For three days it was so dark that the Egyptians could not even see where they were going. By now the Egyptian people were ready for Pharaoh to send the Israelites out of Egypt but Pharaoh still refused.

God had one more plague to send. It would finally convince the Pharaoh to listen to God and release God's people from slavery.

The Last Plague and God's Deliverance

Exodus 11, 12

God sent nine plagues on the Egyptian people to try to convince Pharaoh to let the Israelites out of slavery. God wanted His people free. But even though the nine plagues were terrible, Pharaoh refused to let the people go. God had one more plague to send. He was sure this one would convince Pharaoh because it was awful. God would pass through the land of Egypt and the firstborn son of every family would die, including the oldest son of Pharaoh. Even the firstborn of the animals would die. The Israelites would not be protected from this plague unless they did what God told them to do. His instruction was that each household should kill a lamb and smear its blood on the doorpost of their homes. When God passed through the land and saw the blood on their doorposts, He promised He would pass over their homes and spare their firstborn children and animals. God also said they should have their households packed up and be ready to go when He told them to leave Egypt. God told the people to remember this day of Passover forever as the day that God protected them.

The Israelites packed their things. They killed the lambs and smeared the blood on the doorposts of their homes and they ate the roasted lambs as they were instructed to do. They even asked the Egyptians to give them gold and silver because God told them to do it and the Egyptians gave it to them. The people did everything God told them to do.

At midnight the Lord moved through the land of Egypt. He killed the firstborn son of every family except where He saw the blood of the lamb on the doorposts. Even the son of Pharaoh died. The land of Egypt was filled with the heartbroken cries of families who had lost their sons.

Pharaoh sent for Moses and Aaron during the night. "Get out!" he cried. "Leave Egypt—you and all your people!" All the people of Egypt begged for the Israelites to leave. So Moses led thousands and thousands of Israelites out of Egypt to the land of Canaan which God had promised to them.

31

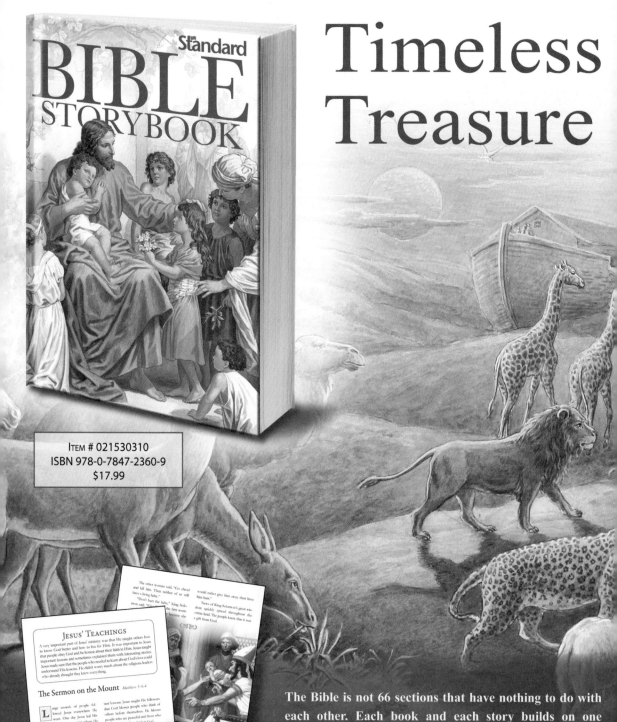